OUR APPOINTMENT WITH LIFE

Our Appointment with Life

SUTRA ON KNOWING THE BETTER WAY
TO LIVE ALONE

Thich Nhat Hanh

PARALLAX PRESS
BERKELEY, CALIFORNIA

Parallax Press
P.O. Box 7355
Berkeley, California 94707
www.parallax.org

Parallax Press is the publishing division of
Unified Buddhist Church, Inc.

All material, except for the introduction, translated
from the Vietnamese by Annabel Laity.
In sutras translated from Chinese, Sanskrit terms are used. In
sutras translated from Pali, Pali terms are used.
Cover and text design by Gopa & Ted2, Inc.
Cover photo copyright © Creative Commons by Rob James

Library of Congress Cataloging-in-Publication Data

Nhât Hanh, Thích, 1926-
   Our Appointment with Life : Sutra on Knowing the Better
Way to Live Alone / Thich Nhat Hanh. — Rev. ed.
      pages cm
   Includes translations from Vietnamese.
   Includes bibliographical references and index.
   ISBN 978-1-935209-79-9 (alk. paper)
   1. Tipitaka. Suttapitaka. Majjhimanikaya. Uparipannasa. Bhad-
dekarattasutta. 2. Religious life—Buddhism. I. Tipitaka. Suttapi-
taka. Majjhimanikaya. Uparipannasa. Bhaddekarattasutta. English.
   II. Title.
   BQ1320.B537N43 2011
   294.3'444—dc22

                                                    2010044898

1 2 3 4 5 / 15 14 13 12 11

Contents

Our appointment with life
is in the present moment.
The place of our appointment
is right here, in this very place.

—THICH NHAT HANH

Introduction
What Does It Mean to Live Alone?

The Sutra on Knowing the Better Way to Live Alone is called the Bhaddekaratta Sutta in Pali. It is number 131 in the Majjhima Nikaya. This important sutra is one of the oldest written teachings on how to live in the present moment.

"Knowing how to live alone" doesn't mean you have to live in solitude in a cave, separated from other people. If we sit alone in a cave, lost in our thinking, we aren't really living alone. "Living alone" means living to have sovereignty over ourselves, to have the freedom that comes from not being dragged away by the past, not living in fear of the future, and not being pulled around by strong emotions caused by the circumstances of the present. When we are master of ourselves, we can grasp the situation as it is, and we're in the best position to handle whatever may arise. When we dwell in mindfulness day and night, then we are truly practicing "the better way to live alone." This is true whether we are surrounded by friends and family, or when we are living a solitary life.

If a doctor tells you, "You have cancer and probably only

have six months to live," you will likely feel completely over-whelmed. The fear, the idea that "I'm going to die in six months," can take away your peace and joy. Before the doctor told you about the cancer you could sit and enjoy your tea, eat your meal, or watch the moon, while now your fear takes away all your joy and freedom.

But the doctor's words can be a bell of mindfulness. We all have six months left to live, or seven months, or ten years. If we can know and accept that death is something that comes to everybody, we will not suffer so much. The doctor who tells us we have six months left to live will also die. Maybe the doctor will die before us. We may be lucky to have six months to live. If we look deeply, we see things that we can't otherwise see. We can get back our freedom from fear and, with that freedom and non-fear, we may live those six months happily.

We are all equal as far as life and death are concerned. Everyone has to die. But before we die, can we live properly? If we live properly, the quality of our last six months can be higher than if we were to live six or sixty more years. If we're caught in the fetters of suffering, our life doesn't have the same meaning it would if we lived in freedom. Knowing that we have to die, we can become determined to live our lives properly and deeply. If we're not able to live with peace, joy, and freedom, then we live as if we're already dead.

In the Sutra on Knowing the Better Way to Live Alone, the Buddha teaches that we must struggle to get back our free-dom, to be able to live the moments of our daily life deeply. If in the moments of our daily life we can have peace and joy, then we can heal the suffering we have in our bodies and our minds. Living deeply in each moment of our life we can be in touch with the wonderful things of life; we can nourish our body and mind with these wonderful elements, and we can embrace and transform our suffering. To live each day of our life deeply is to live a life of wonder, nourishment, and healing. Living like this we can revive our freedom, experience life deeply, give rise to the truth, and have awakened understanding. Our fears, anxieties, sufferings, and sadness will evaporate, and we will become a source of joy and life for ourselves and those around us.

LIVING ALONE IN THE PRESENT MOMENT

There are people who can't see the happiness of the present and think that life was more beautiful in the past. Many of us are caught in this way of thinking. The past is no longer there, but we compare it with the present. Even when we were living those moments in the past we didn't really value them at the time, because in the past we also weren't able to live in the present moment.

There are other people who pursue the past because the past made them suffer. We have all suffered in the past, and those heavy wounds are calling us back: "Come back to the past. You cannot escape me." We can become like sheep running back to the past for it to enclose and imprison us, and make us suffer.

Sometimes when we're sitting with a friend, we can feel abandoned by that friend, because our friend is drowning in the past. He is sitting next to us, but he's not really there. Suppose we find a way to free our friend from the past. We might ask him what he is thinking, or touch him gently in some way to remind him of the present moment. Then our friend may wake up and smile, and be free from the prison of the past.

Sometimes we don't want to go back into the past, but the past grabs hold of us and pulls us back. We have to look directly into the past, smile at it and say, "You can no longer oppress me. I am free of you." The past is just a ghost. We know that the past is a ghost, but we allow the ghost to imprison us.

Some of us run to pursue the future. But the future is another ghost. Why are we afraid of the future? Fear comes from our worry that this or that will or won't happen tomorrow. But the future is something that is not yet here. The future is never here. Once it's here, it's the present.

When we live with a ghost we're not living alone, we're living with another. We eat a meal, but we have the ghost sitting alongside us. When we see a friend sitting with a ghost we can say, "Who are you sitting with?" and perhaps that person will wake up. It's not just the ghosts of the past and the future that like to sit with us. In the present we have infatuations, attachments, feelings of sadness, and projects that take us away from the joy of the present moment. When we live with these things, we are not living alone; we are living with ghosts.

The ghosts of the past and the future take away a lot of our freedom. We can become their slaves. They follow us and condition our life, and order us about. But if we know how to deal with them, we will never fall under their influence. We only have to smile at them. We only need to breathe and come back to our awareness of the present moment and say, "Oh, I know you are a ghost."

Being aware in the present moment does not preclude our thinking about the past or the future. But we must still dwell in the present moment whenever we look deeply into the past or the future, so that we can be aware of any fear or sadness without being overwhelmed by it. According to the teachings of interbeing, the past makes the present, and the present makes the future. Being in touch with the present, we are already in touch with the past and the future.

We're caught by the ghosts of the past and the future because we don't know they're ghosts. We think the past is still right here with us, and we dwell in it. But if we can smile to the ghost of the past, and acknowledge that the past was there, but that now it is gone, then we can have the smile of enlightenment. When we smile like that, it shows we have love for ourselves. We know the past and the future are not our enemies. We know how to live in this moment we are in right now. We need to live our daily moments deeply, as they occur. When we live and know that we are living, this is freedom.

The Sutras

The Elder Sutra*

I heard these words of the Buddha one time when the Lord was staying at the monastery in the Jeta Grove, in the town of Shravasti. At that time there was a monk named Thera (Elder), who always preferred to be alone. Whenever he could, he praised the practice of living alone. He sought alms alone and sat in meditation alone.

One time a group of bhikshus came to the Lord. They paid their respect by prostrating at his feet, stepped to one side, sat down at a distance, and said, "Blessed One, there is an elder by the name of Thera who only wants to be alone. He always praises the practice of living alone. He goes into the village alone to seek alms, returns home from the village alone, and sits in meditation alone."

The Lord Buddha told one of the bhikshus, "Please go to the place where the monk Thera lives and tell him I wish to see him."

The bhikshu obeyed. When the monk Thera heard the Buddha's wish he came without delay, prostrated at the feet

*Samyukta Agama 1071. The equivalent in the Pali Canon is the Theranamo Sutta (Samyutta Nikaya, Sutta number 10). This version is translated from the Chinese by Thich Nhat Hanh.

of the Buddha, stepped to one side, and sat down at a distance. Then the Blessed One asked the monk Thera, "Is it true that you prefer to be alone, praise the life of solitude, go for alms alone, come back from the village alone, and sit in meditation alone?"

The monk Thera replied, "It is true, Blessed One."

Buddha asked the monk Thera, "How do you live alone?"

The monk Thera replied, "I live alone; no one else lives with me. I praise the practice of being alone. I go for alms alone, and I come back from the village alone. I sit in meditation alone. That is all."

The Buddha taught the monk as follows. "It is obvious that you like the practice of living alone. I do not want to deny that, but I want to tell you that there is a more wonderful and profound way to be alone. It is the way of deep observation to see that the past no longer exists and the future has not yet come, and to dwell at ease in the present moment, free from desire. When a person lives in this way, he has no hesitation in his heart. He gives up all anxieties and regrets, lets go of all binding desires, and cuts the fetters which prevent him from being free. This is called 'the better way to live alone.' There is no more wonderful way of being alone than this."

Then the Blessed One recited this gatha:

> Observing life deeply,
>   it is possible to see clearly all that is.
> Not enslaved by anything,
>   it is possible to put aside all craving,

resulting in a life of peace and joy.
This is truly to live alone.

Hearing the Lord's words, the monk Thera was delighted.
He prostrated respectfully to the Buddha and departed.

The Sutra on Knowing the Better Way to Live Alone*

I heard these words of the Buddha one time when the Lord was staying at the monastery in the Jeta Grove, in the town of Shravasti. He called all the monks to him and instructed them, "Bhikkhus!"**

And the bhikkhus replied, "We are here."

The Blessed One taught, "I will teach you what is meant by 'knowing the better way to live alone.' I will begin with an outline of the teaching, and then I will give a detailed explanation. Bhikkhus, please listen carefully."

"Blessed One, we are listening."

The Buddha taught:

> "Do not pursue the past.
> Do not lose yourself in the future.
> The past no longer is.
> The future has not yet come.
> Looking deeply at life as it is

---

*The Bhaddekaratta Sutta (Majjhima Nikaya, Sutta number 131). This version is translated from the Pali by Thich Nhat Hanh.

**Bhikkhu* is the Pali equivalent of the Sanskrit word *bhikshu.*

in the very here and now,
the practitioner dwells
in stability and freedom.
We must be diligent today.
To wait till tomorrow is too late.
Death comes unexpectedly.
How can we bargain with it?
The sage calls a person who
dwells in mindfulness
night and day
'the one who knows
the better way to live alone.'

"Bhikkhus, what do we mean by 'pursuing the past'? When someone considers the way her body was in the past, the way her feelings were in the past, the way her perceptions were in the past, the way her mental formations were in the past, the way her consciousness was in the past; when she considers these things and her mind is burdened by and attached to these things which belong to the past, then that person is pursuing the past.

"Bhikkhus, what is meant by 'not pursuing the past'? When someone considers the way her body was in the past, the way her feelings were in the past, the way her perceptions were in the past, the way her mental formations were in the past, the way her consciousness was in the past; when she considers these things but her mind is neither enslaved by nor attached to these things which belong to the past, then that person is not pursuing the past.

"Bhikkhus, what is meant by 'losing yourself in the future'?

When someone considers the way his body will be in the future, the way his feelings will be in the future, the way his perceptions will be in the future, the way his mental formations will be in the future, the way his consciousness will be in the future; when he considers these things and his mind is burdened by and daydreaming about these things which belong to the future, then that person is losing himself in the future.

"Bhikkhus, what is meant by 'not losing yourself in the future'? When someone considers the way his body will be in the future, the way his feelings will be in the future, the way his perceptions will be in the future, the way his mental formations will be in the future, the way his consciousness will be in the future; when he considers these things but his mind is not burdened by or daydreaming about these things which belong to the future, then he is not losing himself in the future.

"Bhikkhus, what is meant by 'being swept away by the present'? When someone does not study or learn anything about the Awakened one, or the teachings of love and understanding, or the community that lives in harmony and awareness, when that person knows nothing about the noble teachers and their teachings, does not practice these teachings, and thinks, 'This body is myself, I am this body; these feelings are myself, I am these feelings; this perception is myself, I am this perception; this mental formation is myself, I am this mental formation; this consciousness is myself, I am this consciousness,' then that person is being swept away by the present.

"Bhikkhus, what is meant by 'not being swept away by the present'? "When someone studies and learns about the

Awakened One, the teachings of love and understanding, and the community that lives in harmony and awareness, when that person knows about noble teachers and their teachings, practices these teachings, and does not think, 'This body is myself, I am this body; these feelings are myself, I am these feelings; this perception is myself, I am this perception; this mental formation is myself, I am this mental formation; this consciousness is myself, I am this consciousness,' then that person is not being swept away by the present.

"Bhikkhus, I have presented the outline and the detailed explanation of knowing the better way to live alone."

Thus the Buddha taught, and the bhikkhus were delighted to put his teachings into practice.

Commentary on the Sutras

During the time of the Buddha, there was a bhikkhu named Ekavihariya, who liked to live alone. Literally, his name means "One" (*eka*) "Living" (*vihariya*). The Buddha once praised him with this short gatha that appears in the Dhammapada:

> Sitting alone, resting alone,
> going forth alone, without laziness;
> he who understands deeply
> the roots of suffering
> enjoys great peace,
> while dwelling in solitude.

The monk Ekavihariya was well loved and respected by his fellow practitioners.* There was another monk, named Thera (Elder), who also liked to live alone and often spoke highly of the solitary life. However this monk was not praised by his fellow practitioners or by the Buddha. Perhaps Thera wanted to emulate other solitary monks or perhaps he just wanted to practice living alone. But he lived the solitary life only according to the outer form, and his fellow practitioners noticed

---

*Some gathas written by him can be found in the Theragatha (Poems of the Elder Monks), verses 537-546. In these poems he praises the tranquility of living alone.

there was something unbalanced about it. They told the Buddha about him, and the Buddha invited Thera to come see him. The Elder Sutra comes from that encounter.

When Thera presented himself, the Buddha questioned him about his daily life and then offered to show him a much more enjoyable way to live alone, a way that was much more deep and wonderful.

Then the Buddha taught him, "Let go of what is past. Let go of what is not yet. Observe deeply what is happening in the present moment, but do not be attached to it. This is the most wonderful way to live alone."*

The title of the sutra in Pali, Theranamo, means "The One Named Thera." It is possible that after the Buddha taught Thera the contents of this sutra, the other monks, out of respect for him, began to refer to him in the sutra as the Elder, rather than by his prior name.

As the Buddha taught, a person who knows the better way to live alone does not necessarily live isolated from society. To put society at a distance and to live isolated in the forest is no guarantee of being alone. When we are surrounded by the past, worries about the future, or distractions of the present, our vision is muddled and we are never alone. One who knows the better way to live alone can see clearly, even in a crowd of people.

The Buddha discussed the importance of living alone in many sutras, including Migajala Sutra.** In this sutra, a monk

---

*This conversation, so similar to the one in Samyukta Agama 1071, is from the Theranamo Sutta, Samyutta Nikaya, Sutta number 10.
** From the Samyutta Nikaya, Sutta numbers 63 and 64.

named Migajala had heard about the teaching of the better way to live alone and came to ask the Buddha about it.

The Buddha instructed Migajala, "The forms and images which are the objects of our vision can be pleasant, enjoyable, and memorable, and can lead to craving and desire. If a monk is attached to them, then he is bound by them, and he is not alone. He is always with another."

The expression "being with another" is translated from the Pali word *sadutiyavihari*. It is the opposite of "living alone." But when the Buddha used this word, he did not mean that the monk was living with other people. He meant that a monk who is bound by any objects, even objects of consciousness, is actually living with those objects.

The Buddha added, "Indeed, Migajala, if a monk is bound by any fetter like this, even if he lives deep in the forest, in a deserted place without others, and without any outer disturbance, he still lives with another. Why? Because he still has not thrown off the fetters that bind him. Those fetters are the ones with whom he lives."

Buddha taught Migajala that a person who knows the better way to live alone is someone who lives at ease, not bound by the internal formations which are based on the objects of the six senses: form, sound, smell, taste, touch, and the objects of the mind.

The Buddha concluded, "Migajala, if a monk lives like this, even in the center of a village; with monks, nuns, or lay practitioners; among royalty, or high-ranking officials; or with those who practice another way, he is still someone who knows the better way to live alone. He can be said to be living alone because he has freed himself from all attachments."

The Bhaddekaratta gatha was composed by the Buddha to summarize what he had taught Thera and Migajala. The Buddha read this gatha to the monks in the Jetavana monastery and later commented on it for them. The opening paragraphs of the sutra depict the occasion on which the Sutra On Knowing the Better Way to Live Alone was delivered.

The people who were able to hear the Buddha that day were limited to the monks who were present in the Jetavana monastery. Because of the importance of the subject, monks and nuns living elsewhere gradually came to know about the "Knowing the Better Way to Live Alone" gatha. The God of the Forest Hot Springs Sutra tells us, "At that time the Buddha was staying in Rajagriha at the Venuvana monastery. The monk Samiddhi was residing in the nearby forest. One morning after bathing in the hot springs Samiddhi was putting on his robe when a beautiful god appeared, prostrated before him, and asked him if he had ever heard and practiced the "Knowing the Better Way to Live Alone" gatha, saying, "Venerable Samiddhi, you should ask the Buddha to teach us this gatha so that we can put it into practice. I have heard that this gatha contains the deepest meaning of the Buddha's teachings, that it is the basis for the enlightened life, and that it can lead to awakened understanding and *nirvana*." After the god had spoken, he joined his palms and walked clockwise three times around the monk to show his respect.

The monk Samiddhi went to the Buddha. After prostrating to the Awakened One, he told about his encounter with the god and asked the Buddha to teach him the "Knowing the Better Way to Live Alone" gatha. Buddha asked Samiddhi if he knew who the god was. When Samiddhi replied that he did not, Buddha told him the god's name and that he came from the thirty-third heaven. Then Samiddhi and the monks who were present asked the Buddha again to teach them the gatha. Buddha recited it for them:

> Do not pursue the past.
> Do not lose yourself in the future.
> The past no longer is.
> The future has not yet come.
> Looking deeply at life as it is
> in the very here and now,
> the practitioner dwells
> in stability and freedom.
> We must be diligent today.
> To wait until tomorrow is too late.
> Death comes unexpectedly.
> How can we bargain with it?
> The sage calls a person who
> dwells in mindfulness
> night and day
> "the one who knows
> the better way to live alone."

After reciting the gatha, the Buddha left his seat and returned to his hut to meditate. The monks, including Samiddhi, wished to hear an explanation of it, so they went to the elder Kaccana, a senior disciple of the Buddha, recited the gatha to him, and asked if he would comment on it. The monk Kaccana was known to have many excellent qualities. He was often praised by the Buddha for his intelligence, and the monks thought he would be able to offer a penetrating explanation. At first Kaccana hesitated. He suggested that the monks go directly to the Buddha, so that the commentary was from the Teacher himself. But in the end, because the bhikkhus insisted, he agreed to explain the gatha to them. This elder's commentary is the essential content of The God of the Forest Hot Springs Sutra.

After offering his explanation of the gatha, the elder told the monks that if the opportunity presented itself, they should ask Buddha to explain it directly, because his own insight could never be as profound as the insight of the Awakened One.

The bhikkhus, including Samiddhi, did have another audience with the Buddha, and they told the Buddha the explanation of the "Knowing the Better Way to Live Alone" gatha that they had heard from Kaccana. The Buddha began by speaking in praise of the elder: "Excellent. Among my disciples there are those who grasp the meaning of the Dharma and understand its significance. If the teacher recites a gatha and does not have a chance to comment on it, then it is the disciples who must penetrate the meaning of the gatha and give a fuller explanation of the teaching. The Elder Kaccana is a senior bhikkhu. The commentary he gave you shows the true meaning of the gatha and is in accord with the truth of the way things are. You should use it and make it part of your practice."

This exchange took place in Rajagriha, the capital city of Magadha, on the right bank of the Ganges. The account which follows took place further north and west, in the town of Shravasti, the capital of the kingdom of Koshala, on the left bank of the Ganges. That account is given in the Shakyan Hermitage Sutra.

The Shakyan Hermitage had been built by members of the Shakyan clan in the hills not far from Shravasti. This hermitage also had the name "No Problems" or "At Peace." At that time, the bhikkhu Lomasakangiya was staying in the hermitage. One night shortly before daybreak, he stepped outside and spread out a cloth on one of the string cots under the trees. As soon as he began to sit on the cot in the lotus position, a very beautiful god appeared, prostrated before him, and asked if he knew the "Knowing the Better Way to Live Alone" gatha and if he had ever heard a commentary on it. The monk in turn asked the god the same question, and the god replied that he had heard the gatha but he had not yet had the chance to hear the commentary explaining the deep meaning of the gatha. The elder asked, "How is it that you have heard the gatha but have not yet heard the commentary?"

The god explained that at one time, when the Buddha was residing in Rajagriha, he had heard the Buddha recite the gatha, but the Buddha had given no commentary.

Then the god recited the gatha and advised the monk to go and ask the Buddha to explain it. The gatha in this sutra is identical to the one in The God of the Forest Hot Springs Sutra.

After that, the bhikkhu Lomasakangiya went to the Buddha and told him what had happened. At that time, the Buddha was staying in the Jetavana monastery in Shravasti. Having heard the account, the Buddha told Lomasakangiya that the name of the god who had appeared to him was Can-dana (Sandalwood) and that he came from the thirty-third heaven. Then bhikkhu Lomasakangiya requested the Buddha to explain the gatha.

That day, there were many bhikkhus present. The Buddha's commentary on the gatha forms the essence of the Shakyan Hermitage Sutra.*

Another sutra related to the Sutra on Knowing the Better Way to Live Alone is the Sutra Spoken by Ananda.** The Bud-dha delivered this discourse at Sravasti. One night the Venera-ble Ananda asked the monks to assemble in the main Dharma hall of the Jetavana monastery, and he recited and explained the "Knowing the Better Way to Live Alone" gatha. Early the next day, one of the bhikkhus went to see the Buddha and told him about Ananda's Dharma talk. The sutra does not say that the bhikkhu expressed any lack of confidence in the Venerable Ananda, but the sutra does say that after the Buddha heard about the Dharma talk, he sent the bhikkhu to invite Ananda to join them.

When Ananda arrived in the Buddha's room, the Buddha asked him, "Is it true that you recited and gave a talk on the gatha, 'Knowing the Better Way to Live Alone' last night?"

Ananda replied that it was true, and the Buddha asked, "Can you recite it for me and tell me your commentary on it?"

After Ananda recited the gatha and told the Buddha his explanation of it, the Buddha asked Ananda several more

---

*Madhyama Agama 166, which is the equivalent of the Lomasakangiya-Bhad-dekaratta, number 134 in the Majjhima Nikaya.

** Madhyama Agama 167, equivalent to the Ananda-Bhaddekaratta in the Pali Canon, Majjhima Nikaya 132.

questions. The main part of the Sutra Spoken by Ananda is comprised of the answers given by Ananda to the Buddha's questions. When he heard Ananda's answers, he praised him saying, "Excellent! Among my disciples there are those who have the insight to understand the essential significance of the teachings."

Buddha praised Ananda in the way that he had praised Kaccana. On that day there were many bhikkhus present, among them the bhikkhu who had told the Buddha about Ananda's Dharma talk. Perhaps the Buddha spoke those words to assure the monks that the Venerable Ananda's grasp of the Dharma was as firm as Kaccana's and that the bhikkhus could make Ananda's teachings a part of their practice.

Part Three: Putting the Teachings of the Buddha into Practice

To live alone does not mean to reject the world and society. The Buddha said that living alone means living in the present moment, deeply observing what is happening. If we do that, we will not be dragged into the past or swept away into thoughts about the future. The Buddha said that if we cannot live in the present moment, even if we are alone in the deepest forest, we are not really alone. He said that if we are fully alive in the present moment, even if we are in a crowded urban area, we can still be said to be living alone.

It is important to practice in a community. A Vietnamese proverb goes: "Soup is to a meal what friends are to the practice." When we practice in a community, we can learn from its members, and take refuge in our communal practice. We need to discover the way of being alone in a practice community.

The monk Thera was part of a practice community, but he was determined to live alone. He believed in the idea of a solitary life, because he had at some time heard the Buddha praising the practice of living alone. So he kept his distance from everyone else. He begged for alms alone, he returned alone, he ate alone, and he meditated alone. He was like a drop of oil in a bowl of water, unable to mix with his fellow practitioners. The other monastics felt something was not right with his practice, and they expressed their concern to the Buddha.

The Buddha was very kind. He did not criticize Thera. He

only said that Thera's way of living alone was not the best way of doing so. Because there were many other monks present at the time and they could benefit from the teaching, the Buddha took the opportunity to teach Thera that the better way of living alone is to associate with the other monastics, to learn from them and take refuge in them.

There were bhikkhus who were the opposite of Thera, who would always gather in small groups and fritter away their time chatting and joking. Their conversations were not about the teachings, and the Buddha frequently reprimanded them. There are stories throughout the sutras in which the Buddha advises or chides the bhikkhus who act in a noisy and undisciplined way, not knowing how to keep body and mind in check, not knowing how to spend their time usefully in practicing walking and sitting meditation and observing deeply things as they are in the present moment.*

When I first became a monk, my master gave me a copy of the book, *Encouraging Words of Master Guishan.* I will never forget the sentences in which Master Guishan reprimands practitioners who, after the midday meal, gather in small groups and talk about meaningless things. Guishan's words of advice have often come back to me and served as a reminder:

When you receive food offered by donors, wouldn't it be better to meditate on the food than to think that as a monk you deserve to receive it? When you

---

* In the Pali Canon, see the Nagita Sutta, Anguttara Nikaya chapters 5.30, 6.42, 8.86. In the Chinese Canon, see Samyukta Agama 1250 and 1251.

finish eating, if you sit around talking idly, it will increase everyone's suffering later on. How many lifetimes do you plan to chase after worldly matters without looking deeply at where your life is going? Time flies like an arrow, yet you are still attached to the pleasure of the offerings you receive, and you still think that money and possessions will provide you security. The Buddha taught his monks to be satisfied with just enough food, clothing, and shelter. Why would a monk or a nun spend so much time craving these things? By the time you wake up, your hair will be white. Listen to the wise ones. They did not become monks and nuns just to have some food to eat and a robe to wear.*

When we live in a practice community, there should always be at least one or two people who serve as role models. Sometimes we only need to watch them standing, walking, speaking, or smiling in mindfulness, and we feel steady in our own practice. The fact that we know "the better way to live alone" does not prevent us from enjoying and benefitting from the presence of such people. On the contrary, it is because we know "the better way to live alone" that we have the ability to observe them deeply and appreciate them.

To be in touch does not mean just to talk with the other person. When we are in touch with the blue sky, for example, the white clouds, the green willow, or the rose, we do

*For the full text, see Thich Nhat Hanh, *Stepping Into Freedom* (Parallax Press, 1997).

not communicate with them only in words. We recognize and accept these things, and feel their warmth. Confidence springs up in us, and we learn a lot from their presence. In this way we are able to profit from the third jewel, the practice community.

If we practice "the better way of living alone," and we spend most of our time quietly practicing walking and sitting meditation, our presence will make a real contribution to the community. Unlike the monk Thera or the monks who gather after meals to talk about things that are not important, every step we make adds to the quality and stability of the practice in the community. We are like Shariputra, Kashyapa, Badhya, or Kimbila—all students of the Buddha. Seeing us, the Buddha will be satisfied and smile. The Buddha knows that if every individual in the community knows how to live alone, the quality of life in the community will be excellent. When all the members of the community contribute to that quality, the community has a strong foundation, and many people can benefit from it. To live alone means to live in mindfulness. It does not mean to isolate oneself from society. If we know the better way to live alone, we can be in real touch with people and society, and we will know what to do and what not to do to be of help.

AWAKE AND ALONE

If we live in forgetfulness, if we lose ourselves in the past or in the future, if we allow ourselves to be tossed about by our desires, anger, and ignorance, we will not be able to live each moment of our life deeply. We will not be in contact with what is happening in the present moment, and our relations with others will become shallow and impoverished.

Some days we may feel hollow, exhausted, and joyless, not really our true selves. On such days, even if we try to be in touch with others, our efforts will be in vain. The more we try, the more we fail. When this happens, we should stop trying to be in touch with what is outside of ourselves and come back to being in touch with ourselves. We should "be alone." This is a time to practice conscious breathing, observing deeply what is going on inside and around us. We can accept all the phenomena we observe, say hello to them, and smile at them. We do well to do simple things, like walking or sitting meditation, washing our clothes, cleaning the floor, making tea, and cleaning the bathroom in mindfulness. If we do these things, we will restore the richness of our spiritual life.

The Buddha was someone who lived an awakened life, dwelling constantly in the present moment in a relaxed and steady way. There was always a richness about him—a richness of freedom, joy, understanding, and love. Whether he was seated on a rocky crag of Vulture Peak, in the shade of the bamboo groves of Venuvana monastery, or under the thatched roof of his hut in Jetavana, Buddha was Buddha, unagitated, content, and of few words. Everyone could see that his presence contributed greatly to the harmony and stability of the community. The monks and nuns were affected just by knowing he was nearby. Many students of the Buddha, including hundreds of senior disciples, inspired similar confidence in those who observed them. King Prasenajit of Koshala once told the Buddha that what gave him so much confidence in the Buddha was the unhurried, calm, and joyful way of life of the monks and nuns who were practicing under his guidance.

If we live in mindfulness, we are no longer poor, because our practice of living in the present moment makes us rich in joy, peace, understanding, and love. Even when we encounter someone poor in spirit, we can look deeply and discover that person's rich layers.

When we watch a documentary or read a book or look at someone's painting or sculpture, if we are already poor in heart and mind, and weak in mindfulness, what we are reading or looking at may irritate us and make us feel even more poor. But if we are rich in mindfulness, we will discover what lies in the depths of that art. We may be able to see deeply into the inner world of the person who made it. Looking with the eyes of an art critic, we can see things that most people do not see, and even a bad movie or book or sculpture can teach us. Maintaining full awareness of each detail of the present moment, we are able to profit from it. This is the better way to live alone.

TIED UP INSIDE

The "Knowing the Better Way To Live Alone" gatha begins with the line: "Do not pursue the past." To "pursue the past" means to regret what has already come and gone. We regret the loss of the beautiful things of the past which we can no longer find in the present. Buddha commented on this line as follows: "When someone thinks how his body was in the past, how his feelings were in the past, how his perceptions were in the past, how his mental formations were in the past, how his consciousness was in the past, when he thinks like that and gives rise to a mind which is enslaved by those things which belong to the past, then that person is pursuing the past."

Buddha taught that we should not pursue the past "because the past no longer is." When we are lost in thoughts about the past, we lose the present. Life exists only in the present moment. To lose the present is to lose life. The Buddha's meaning is very clear: we must say goodbye to the past so that we may return to the present. To return to the present is to be in touch with life.

What dynamics in our consciousness compel us to go back and live with the images of the past? These forces are made up of internal formations (Sanskrit: *samyojana*), mental formations which arise in us and bind us. Things we see, hear, smell, taste, touch, imagine, or think can all give rise to internal formations—desire, irritation, anger, confusion, fear, anxiety, suspicion, and so on. Internal formations are present in the depths of the consciousness of each of us.

Internal formations influence our consciousness and our everyday behavior. They cause us to think, say, and do things that we may not even be aware of. Because they compel us in this way, they are also called fetters, because they bind us to acting in certain ways.

The commentaries usually mention nine kinds of internal formations: desire, hatred, pride, ignorance, stubborn views, attachment, doubt, jealousy, and selfishness. Among these, the fundamental internal formation is ignorance, the lack of clear seeing. Ignorance is the raw material out of which the other internal formations are made. Although there are nine internal formations, because "desire" is always listed first, it is often used to represent all the internal formations. In the Kaccana-Bhaddekaratta, the monk Kaccana explains:

> My friends, what is meant by dwelling in the past? Someone thinks, "In the past my eyes were like that and the form (with which my eyes were in contact) was like that," and thinking like this, he is bound by desire. Bound by desire, there is a feeling of longing. This feeling of longing keeps him dwelling in the past.

Kaccana's commentary could make us think that the only internal formation holding one in the past is desire. But when Kaccana refers to "desire," he is using it to represent all the internal formations—hatred, doubt, jealousy, and so forth. All of these tie us and hold us back in the past.

Sometimes we only have to hear the name of someone who has wronged us in the past, and our internal formations from that time automatically take us back into the past, and we relive the suffering. The past is the home ground of both painful and happy memories. Being absorbed in the past is a way of being dead to the present moment. It is not easy to drop the past and return to living in the present. When we try to do it, we have to resist the force of the internal formations in us. We have to learn to transform our internal formations, so that we will be free to be attentive to the present moment.

Standing Firmly

The present contains the past. When we understand how our internal formations cause conflicts in us, we can see how the past is in the present moment, and we will no longer be overwhelmed by the past. When the Buddha said, "Do not pursue the past," he was telling us not to be overwhelmed by the past. He did not mean that we should stop looking at the past in order to observe it deeply. When we review the past and observe it deeply, if we are standing firmly in the present, we are not overwhelmed by it. The materials of the past which make up the present become clear when they express themselves in the present. We can learn from them. If we observe these materials deeply, we can arrive at a new understanding of them. That is called "looking again at something old in order to learn something new."

If we know that the past also lies in the present, we understand that we are able to change the past by transforming the present. The ghosts of the past, which follow us into the present, also belong to the present moment. To observe them deeply, recognize their nature, and transform them, is to transform the past. The ghosts of the past are very real. They are the internal formations in us, which are sometimes quietly asleep, while at other times they awaken suddenly and forcefully. There is the Sanskrit term *anushaya*. *Anu* means "along with." *Shaya* means "lying down." We could translate anushaya as "latent tendency." The internal formations continue to be with us, but they are lying asleep in the depths of our consciousness. We call them ghosts, but they are present in a very real way. According to the Vijñanavada school of Buddhism, anushaya are seeds which lie in every-one's subconscious (*alaya*). An important part of the work of observation meditation is to be able to recognize the *anu-shaya* when they manifest, observe them deeply, and trans-form them.

FUTURE GHOSTS

Sometimes, because the present is so difficult, we give our attention to the future, hoping that the situation will improve in the future. Imagining the future will be better, we are bet-ter able to accept the suffering and hardship of the present. But at other times, thinking about the future may cause us a lot of fear and anxiety, and yet we cannot stop doing it. The reason we continue to think about the future, even when we do not want to, is due to the presence of internal formations. Although not yet here, the future is already producing ghosts which haunt us. In fact, these ghosts are not produced by the future or the past. It is our consciousness which creates them. The past and the future are creations of our consciousness.

The energies behind our thinking about the future are our hopes, dreams, and anxieties. Our hopes can be the result of our sufferings and failures. Because the present does not bring us happiness, we allow our minds to travel into the future. We hope that in the future, the situation will be brighter: "When someone considers how his body will be in the future, how his feelings will be in the future, how his mental formations will be in the future, how his consciousness will be in the future..." Thinking in this way can give us the courage to accept failure and suffering in the present. The poet Tru Vu said that the future is the vitamin for the present. Hope brings us back some of the joys of life that we have lost.

We all know that hope is necessary for life. But according to Buddhism, hope can be an obstacle. If we invest our mind in the future, we will not have enough mental energy to face and transform the present. Naturally we have the right to make plans for the future, but making plans for the future does not mean to be being swept away by daydreams. While we are making plans, our feet are firmly planted in the present. We can only build the future from the raw materials of the present.

The essential teaching of Buddhism is to be free of all desire for the future in order to come back with all our heart and mind into the present. To realize awakening means to arrive at a deep and full insight into reality, which is in the present moment. In order to return to the present and to be face to face with what is happening, we must look deeply into the heart of what is and experience its true nature. When we do so, we experience the deep understanding which can release us from suffering and darkness.

According to Buddhism, hell, paradise, *samsara*, and *nirvana* are all here in the present moment. To return to the present moment is to discover life and to realize the truth. All the Awakened Ones of the past have come to Awakening in the present moment. All the Awakened Ones of the present and the future will realize the fruit of Awakening in the present also. Only the present moment is real: "The past no longer is, and the future has not yet come."

If we do not stand firmly in the present moment, we may feel ungrounded when we look at the future. We may think that in the future we will be alone, with no place of refuge and no one to help us. "When someone considers how his body will be in the future, how his feelings will be in the future, how his mental formations will be in the future, how his consciousness will be in the future..." Such concerns about the future bring about unease, anxiety, and fear, and do not help us at all in taking care of the present moment. They just make our way of dealing with the present weak and confused. There is a Confucian saying that a person who does not know how to plan for the distant future will be troubled and perplexed by the near future. This is meant to remind us to care for the future, but not to be anxious and fearful about it. The best way of preparing for the future is to take good care of the present, because we know that if the present is made up of the past, then the future will be made up of the present. All we need to be responsible for is the present moment. Only the present is within our reach. To care for the present is to care for the future.

SMILING WITHIN

When we think about the past, feelings of regret or shame may arise. When we think about the future, feelings of desire or fear may come up. But all of these feelings arise in the present moment, and they all affect the present moment. Most of the time, their effect does not contribute to our happiness or joy. We have to learn how to face these feelings. The main thing we need to remember is that the past and the future are both in the present, and if we take hold of the present moment, then we also transform the past and the future.

How can we transform the past? In the past we may have said or done something destructive or harmful, and now we regret it. According to Buddhist psychology, regret is an "indeterminate emotion." This means that it can be either constructive or destructive. When we know that something we have said or done has caused harm, we may give rise to a mind of repentance, vowing that in the future we will not repeat the same mistake. In this case, our feeling of regret has a wholesome effect. If, on the other hand, the feeling of regret continues to disturb us, making it impossible for us to concentrate on anything else, taking all the peace and joy out of our lives, then that feeling of regret has an unwholesome effect.

When regret becomes unwholesome, we should first distinguish whether the cause was based on something we did or said, or on something we failed to do or say. If in the past, we said or did something destructive, we can call that an "error of commission." We did or said something with a lack of mindfulness, and it caused harm. Sometimes we commit an "error of omission." We did harm by not saying or doing what needed to be said or done, and that brought us regret and sorrow. Our lack of mindfulness was there, and its results are still present. Our pain, shame, and regret are an important part of that result. If we observe the present deeply and take hold of it, we can transform it. We do so by means of mindfulness, determination, and correct actions and speech. All these come about in the present moment. When we transform the present in this way, we also transform the past, and at the same time, we build the future.

If we say that all is lost, everything is destroyed, or the

suffering has already happened, we do not see that the past has become the present. Of course, the suffering has already been caused and the wound of that suffering can touch our very soul, but instead of lamenting about or suffering from what we have done in the past, we should take hold of the present and transform it. The traces of a bad drought can only be erased by a bountiful rainfall, and rain can only fall in the present moment.

Buddhist repentance is based on the understanding that wrongdoing originates in the mind. There is a gatha of repentance:

> All wrongdoing arises from the mind.
> If mind is purified, what trace of wrong is left?
> After repentance, my heart is light
> like the white clouds that have always floated over the
> ancient forest in freedom.

Because of our lack of mindfulness, because our mind was obscured by desire, anger, and jealousy, we acted wrongly. That is what is meant by "All wrongdoing arises from the mind." But if the wrongdoing arose from our mind, it can also be transformed within our mind. If our mind is transformed, then the objects perceived by our mind will also be transformed. Such transformation is available if we know how to return to the present moment. Once we have transformed our mind, our heart will be as light as a floating cloud, and we become a source of peace and joy for ourselves and others. Yesterday, perhaps out of foolishness or anger, we said something which made our mother sad. But today our mind is transformed and our heart light, and we can see our mother smiling at us, even if she is no longer alive. If we can smile within ourselves, our mother can also smile with us.

If we can transform the past, we can also transform the future. Our anxieties and fears for the future make the present dark. There is no doubt that the future will be black too, because we know that the future is made up of the present. Taking care of the present is the best way to take care of the future. Sometimes, because we are so concerned about what will happen the next day, we toss and turn all night, unable to sleep. We worry that if we cannot sleep during the night, we will be tired the next day and unable to perform to the best of our ability. The more we worry, the more difficult it is for us to sleep. Our worries and fears for the future destroy the present. But if we stop thinking about tomorrow and just stay in bed and follow our breathing, really enjoying the opportunity we have to rest, not only will we savor the moments of peace and joy under the warm blankets, but we will fall asleep quite easily and naturally. That kind of sleep is a big help for making the next day a success.

When we hear that the forests of our planet are diseased and dying so rapidly, we may feel anxious. We are concerned for the future, because we are aware of what is happening in the present moment. Our awareness can motivate us to do something to halt the destruction of our environment. Obviously, our concern for the future is different from worry and anxiety which only drain us. We have to know how to enjoy the presence of beautiful, healthy trees in order to be able to do something to protect and preserve them.

When we throw a banana peel into the compost heap, if

we are mindful, we know that the peel will become com-post and be reborn as a tomato or as lettuce in just a few months. But when we throw a plastic bag into the garbage, thanks to our awareness, we know that a plastic bag will not become a tomato or a salad very quickly. Some kinds of gar-bage need four or five hundred years to decompose. Nuclear waste needs a quarter of a million years before it stops being harmful and returns to the soil. Living in the present moment in an awakened way, looking after the present moment with all our heart, we will not do things which destroy the future. That is the most concrete way to do what is constructive for the future.

In our everyday life, we may also produce poisons for our minds, and these poisons destroy not only us but also those who live with us, in the present and in the future too. Bud-dhism talks about three poisons: desire, hatred, and igno-rance. In addition, there are other poisons whose capacity to do harm is very great: jealousy, prejudice, pride, suspicion, and obstinacy.

In our day-to-day relationships with ourselves, others, and our environment, any or all of these poisons can manifest, blaze up, and destroy our peace and joy, as well as the peace and joy of those around us. These poisons can linger and pol-lute our minds, causing bitter consequences in the future. So to live in the present moment is also to accept and face these poisons as they arise, manifest, and return to the unconscious, and to practice observation meditation in order to transform them. This is a Buddhist practice. To live in the present is also to see the wonderful and wholesome things in order to nourish and protect them. Happiness is the direct result of facing things and being in touch. That happiness is the material from which a beautiful future is constructed.

LIFE IS A PATH

To return to the present is to be in contact with life. Life can be found only in the present moment, because "the past no longer is" and "the future has not yet come." Buddhahood, liberation, awakening, peace, joy, and happiness can only be found in the present moment. Our appointment with life is in the present moment. The place of our appointment is right here, in this very place.

According to the Avatamsaka Sutra, time and space are not separate. Time is made up of space, and space is made up of time. When we speak about spring, we usually think of time, but spring is also space. When it is spring in Europe, it is winter in Australia.

When we have a tea mediation, those who attend breathe in and out and recite the following gatha together before taking the first sip of tea:

> This cup of tea in my two hands—
> mindfulness is held uprightly.
> My mind and body dwell
> in the very here and now.

When we drink tea in mindfulness, we practice coming back to the present moment to live our life right here. When our mind and our body are fully in the present moment, then the steaming cup of tea appears clearly to us. We know it is a wonderful aspect of existence. At that time we are really in contact with the cup of tea. It is only at times like this that life is really present.

Peace, joy, liberation, awakening, happiness, Buddhahood, the source—everything we long for and seek after can only be found in the present moment. To abandon the present moment in order to look for these things in the future is to throw away the substance and hold on to the shadow. In Buddhism, aimlessness (*apranihita*) is taught as a way to help the practitioner stop pursuing the future and return wholly to the present. Aimlessness is sometimes called wishlessness, and it is one of the "three doors of liberation." (The other two are emptiness and signlessness.) To be able to stop pursuing the future allows us to realize that all the wonderful things we seek are present in us, in the present moment. Life is not a particular place or a destination. Life is a path. To practice walking meditation is to go without needing to arrive. Every step can bring us peace, joy, and liberation. That is why we walk in the spirit of aimlessness. There is no way to liberation, peace, and joy; peace and joy are themselves the way. Our appointment with the Buddha, with liberation, with happiness, is here and now. We should not miss this appointment.

Buddhism teaches a way of breathing which gives us the capacity of making body and mind one in order to be face to face with life. This is called "oneness of body and mind." That is why every meditator begins by practicing the Sutra on the Full Awareness of Breathing (Anapanasati Sutta).

But to come back to the present does not mean to be carried away by what is happening in the present. The sutra teaches us to observe life deeply and be in touch with the present moment, and see all the sufferings and the wonders of the present. Yet we must do so in mindfulness, maintaining a high degree of awareness in order not to be carried away by, or caught in, desire for or aversion to what is happening in the present.

> Looking deeply at life as it is
> in the very here and now,
> the practitioner dwells
> in stability and freedom.

"Stability and freedom" refer to the contentment and tranquility of not being carried away by anything whatsoever. Stability and ease are two characteristics of nirvana. The Pali version of this verse uses two terms, *asamkuppam* and *asamhiram*. Asamkuppam means "unwavering, unshakable, immovable, unexcitable." Sanghadeva, the monk and translator of the Madhyama Agama, translates it as "firm and unwavering." The monk Dharmapala translates it as "stable." Asamhiram means, literally, "not folded together, not restrained, not collected, not carried away by anything." Sanghadeva translated asamhiram into Chinese as "non-existing" (*wu yu*), which is not exact. Dharmapala, in The Elder Sutra, translated asamhiram as "not fettered." "Fettered" here means "imprisoned." So "not fettered" means "not caught" or "in freedom."

Being in contact with life in the present moment, we observe deeply what is. Then we are able to see the impermanent and selfless nature of all that is. Impermanence and selflessness are not negative aspects of life but the very foundations on which life is built. Impermanence is the constant transformation of things. Without impermanence, there can be no life. Self-lessness is the interdependent nature of all things. Without interdependence, nothing could exist. Without the sun, the clouds, and the Earth, the tulip could not be. We often feel sad about the impermanence and selflessness of life, because we forget that without impermanence and selflessness, life cannot be. To be aware of impermanence and selflessness does not take away the joy of being alive. On the contrary, it adds healthiness, stability, and freedom. It is because people cannot see the impermanent and selfless nature of things that they suffer. They take what is impermanent as permanent and what is selfless as having a self.

Looking deeply into a rose, we can see its impermanent nature quite clearly. At the same time, we can see its beauty and value its preciousness. Because we perceive its fragile and impermanent nature, we may see that flower as even more beautiful and precious. The more fragile something is, the more beautiful and precious it is—for example, a rainbow, a sunset, a cereus cactus flowering by night, a falling star. Looking at the sun rising over Vulture Peak, at the town of Vesali, at a field of ripe, golden rice, the Buddha saw their beauty and told Ananda so.

Seeing deeply the impermanent nature of those beautiful things, their transformation and disappearance, the Buddha did not suffer or despair. We, too, by observing deeply and seeing impermanence and selflessness in all that is, can overcome despair and suffering and experience the preciousness of the miracles of everyday life—a glass of clear water, a cool breeze, a step taken in ease and freedom. These are wonderful things, although they are impermanent and selfless.

Life is suffering, but it is also wonderful. Sickness, old age, death, accidents, starvation, unemployment, and natural disasters cannot be avoided in life. But, if our understanding is deep and our mind free, we can accept these things with tranquility, and the suffering will already be greatly lessened. This is not to say we should close our eyes before suffering. By being in contact with suffering, we give rise to and nourish our natural love and compassion. Suffering becomes the element which nourishes our love and compassion, and so we are not afraid of it. When our heart is filled with love and compassion, we will act in ways to help relieve the suffering of others.

If the human species has been able to make any progress, it is because of our heart of love and compassion. We need to learn from compassionate beings how to develop the practice of deep observation for the sake of others. Then others will be able to learn from us the way to live in the present and see the impermanent and selfless nature of all that is. This insight will lighten suffering.

Fear of the unexpected leads many people to live a constricted and anxious life. No one can know in advance the misfortunes which may happen to us and our loved ones, but if we learn to live in an awakened way, living deeply every moment of our life, treating those who are close to us with gentleness and understanding, then we will have nothing to regret when something happens to us or to them. Living in the present moment, we are able to be in touch with life's wonderful, refreshing, and health-giving phenomena, which allow us to heal the wounds in ourselves. Every day we become more wonderful, fresh, and healthy.

PEACE, FREEDOM, AND JOY

To practice a life of deep observation according to the teachings of the Buddha is to have a life of peace, freedom, and joy, and to realize complete liberation. The "Knowing the Better Way to Live Alone" gatha reminds us that we cannot avoid death and advises us to be diligent in the practice today, for tomorrow it will be too late. Death comes unexpectedly, and there is no way to bargain with it. If we live observing everything deeply in the present moment, we learn to live in peace and joy with freedom and stability. If we continue to practice diligently in this way, peace, joy, and stability will grow every day until we realize complete liberation. When there is complete liberation, death can no longer harm us.

A life like this will bring joy to our dear ones and others. The material of stability and release is also the element of liberation. Liberation is the fruit of deep observation which leads to the realization of the impermanent and selfless nature of all that is. By observing at a deep level, we can defeat death, because the observation of impermanence can lead us to transcend the boundaries of birth and death. When we look at all that is in the universe and all those dear to us, we see that there is nothing eternal and unchanging that we can call "I" or "self."

TRANSCENDING BIRTH AND DEATH

We often think that birth means that what did not exist comes into existence, and that death means that which exists ceases to exist. When we look deeply at things, we see that this idea about birth and death is mistaken in many respects. No phenomenon whatsoever can come into existence out of nothing, and no phenomenon which exists can become nothing. Things are ceaselessly transforming. The cloud does not die; it only becomes rain. The rain is not born; it is only the transformation and continuation of the cloud. Leaves, a pair of shoes, joy, and sorrow all conform to this principle of no-birth and no-death. To think that after death we no longer exist is a narrow view which in Buddhism is called the "nihilistic view." The narrow view that after death we continue to exist without changing is called the "view of permanence." Reality transcends both permanence and annihilation.

The Buddha taught us to look directly into the elements which combine together to constitute our body, in order to see the nature of these elements and transcend the idea of "self"—whether it is the idea of a permanent, indestructible self, or the idea of a self subject to complete annihilation after we die. The sutra says: "Someone who studies and learns about the Awakened One, the teachings of love and understanding, and the community which lives in harmony and awareness, who knows about noble teachers and their teachings, practices these teachings, and does not think, 'This body is myself, I am this body; these feelings are myself, I am these feelings; this perception is myself, I am this perception; this mental formation is myself, I am this mental formation; this consciousness is myself, I am this consciousness,' then that person does not go back to the past, does not think ahead to the future, and is not being swept away by the present."

The five elements which combine together to become the thing we call self are form (the body), feelings, perceptions,

mental formations, and consciousness. If we look penetrat-
ingly into the substance of these elements and see their
impermanent and interdependent nature, we naturally see
that there is no entity we can call "self." All five elements are
constantly transforming. They are never born and never die.
There is no element that goes from nothingness into existence, nor any element which goes from existence into nothingness. The thing which we think of as "I" is not born and
does not die. We do not identify "I" with the body, whether
that body is developing or degenerating, nor with the feelings which change at every moment. Similarly, we do not
identify with our perceptions and our consciousness. We are
not bound or limited by these five elements. We see that if
these elements really are not born or destroyed, then we need
no longer be oppressed by death. This insight enables us to
transcend birth and death.

When the sutra refers to someone who "practices according to the teachings of the Noble Ones," it means someone
who lives in the present and observes deeply in order to see
life's impermanent and selfless nature. The Buddha taught
that "we must practice diligently today, for tomorrow will be
too late; death comes unexpectedly and there is no bargain-
ing with it." Observing deeply, we can realize the birthless
and deathless nature of things, and there is nothing more
which can frighten us, not even death. We directly overcome
birth and death when, by deep observation and realization of
impermanence and selflessness, we pierce through false ideas
about the nature of existence. Once we overcome death, we
no longer need to "bargain with death." We can smile, take
the hand of death, and go for a walk together.

The life called the "brahma-faring life" of a monk or a nun can lead to the realization of the birthless and deathless nature of all that is. That realization is the substance of liberation. That is why in the Kaccana-Bhaddekaratta Sutra it is emphasized that the practice of living alone is the basis of the brahma-faring life of a monk or a nun. It is also the basis of life for all of us.

Appendix

Appendix:
The Bhaddekaratta Gatha in Other Sutras

Knowing the better way to live alone shines light on the essence of living in an awakened way as taught by the Buddha. The sutra teaches us to let go of the past and the future, and to live mindfully in order to look deeply and discover the true nature of all that is taking place in the present moment.

THE BHADDEKARATTA GATHA IN THE PALI CANON

The Bhaddekaratta gatha became well known and is found in many other sutras in both the Pali Canon and the Chinese Canon.

In the Pali Canon, I have come across four suttas with the "Bhaddekaratta" gatha, all in the Majjhima Nikaya. The first is the Bhaddekaratta Sutta (number 131). The second is the Ananda-Bhaddekaratta Sutta (number 132), which is the equivalent of the Sutra Spoken by Ananda. The third is the Mahakaccana-Bhaddekaratta Sutta (number 133), equivalent to The God of the Forest Hot Springs Sutra. The fourth is the Lomasakangiya-Bhaddekaratta Sutta (M134), equivalent to the Shakyan Hermitage Sutra.

Besides the four Pali suttas and Chinese sutras mentioned above, the subject of living alone is referred to in many other places in the canons, in detail in the Theranamo and the Migajala sutras, although the Bhaddekaratta gatha is not specifically quoted.

The terms *ekavihari* (one who lives alone) and *sadutiyavihari* (one who lives with another) in the Migajala Sutta are easy to understand and accept. But the term *bhaddekaratta* is difficult to translate. Dharmanandi, who translated the Samyukta Agama into Chinese, did not understand this compound word, so he just transcribed it into Chinese characters and used it as the title of the gatha.*

A number of Buddhist masters of the Southern Tradition understand *ekaratta* as "one night" and translate Bhaddekaratta as "A Good Night for Meditation." Judging from the content of the sutra, I believe this translation is not correct. *Bhadda* means "good" or "ideal." *Eka* means "one" or "alone." *Ratta* means "to like." The contemporary Buddhist scholar Bhikkhu Nanananda translates the title as "The Ideal Lover of Solitude." After much reflection, I think that "Knowing the Better Way to Live Alone" is closer to the original meaning of the sutra.

---

*Master Dharmapala translated bhaddekaratta as *xian shan*. *Xian* means "virtuous" or "able," *shan* means "good," "good at," or "skillful." These two words translate *bhadda* and *ratta*. But the part *eka*, "alone," which lies between badha and ratta, has been overlooked, although it is fundamental to the meaning of the compound.

The Bhaddekaratta Gatha in the Chinese Canon

In the Madhyama Agama there are three sutras which quote this gatha. The first is The God of the Forest Hot Springs Sutra (number 165), in which the poem is quoted four times. The second is The Shakyan Hermitage Sutra (number 166), in which the gatha is quoted three times. The third sutra is the Sutra Spoken by Ananda (number 167), in which the gatha is quoted once. The following is the translation of the gatha as it appears in the three sutras:

Do not think of the past.
Do not worry about the future.
Things of the past have died.
The future has not arrived.
What is happening in the present
should be observed deeply.
The Wise Ones live according to this
and dwell in stability and freedom.
If one practices the teachings
of the Wise Ones,
why should one be afraid of death?
If we do not understand this,
there is no way to avoid
the great pain of the final danger.
To practice diligently day and night,
one should regularly recite
the Bhaddekaratta Gatha.

The following Bhaddekaratta Gatha is seen in the translation of the Great Reverence Sutra, which is no. 77 in the Taisho Revised Tripitaka.

> Not thinking about the past,
> not seeking something in the future—
> the past has already died,
> the future is not in our hands—
> we should observe deeply
> and contemplate
> what is in the present moment.
> The person who constantly practices
> the way of the wise ones
> has awakened understanding.
> Diligently practicing,
> without wavering, and
> released from care,
> what does he fear at the time of death?
> If he does not practice diligently,
> how can he overcome death and its armies?
> Truly we should practice
> according to this wonderful gatha.

Parallax Press, a nonprofit organization, publishes books on engaged Buddhism and the practice of mindfulness by Thich Nhat Hanh and other authors. All of Thich Nhat Hanh's work is available at our online store and in our free catalog. For a copy of the catalog, please contact:

Parallax Press
P.O. Box 7355
Berkeley, CA 94707
Tel: (510) 525-0101
www.parallax.org

Monastics and laypeople practice the art of mindful living in the tradition of Thich Nhat Hanh at retreat communities in France and the United States. To reach any of these communities, or for information about individuals and families joining for a practice period, please contact:

Plum Village
13 Martineau
33580 Dieulivol, France
www.plumvillage.org

Blue Cliff Monastery
3 Mindfulness Road
Pine Bush, NY 12566
www.bluecliffmonastery.org

Deer Park Monastery
2499 Melru Lane
Escondido, CA 92026
www.deerparkmonastery.org

The *Mindfulness Bell,* a Journal of the Art of Mindful Living in the Tradition of Thich Nhat Hanh, is published three times a year by Plum Village. To subscribe or to see the worldwide directory of Sanghas, visit www.mindfulnessbell.org.